HERE'S WHERE HISTORY HAPPENED!

INDEPENDENCE HALL

BY JANEY LEVY

Gareth Stevens PUBLISHING

Please visit our website, www.garethstevens.com. For a free color catalog of all our high-quality books, call toll free 1-800-542-2595 or fax 1-877-542-2596.

Library of Congress Cataloging-in-Publication Data

Names: Levy, Janey, author.
Title: Independence Hall / Janey Levy.
Description: [Buffalo, New York] : Gareth Stevens Publishing, [2025] | Series: Here's where history happened! | Includes bibliographical references and index. | Audience: Grades 2-3
Identifiers: LCCN 2023053528 (print) | LCCN 2023053529 (ebook) | ISBN 9781482466386 (library binding) | ISBN 9781482466379 (paperback) | ISBN9781482466393 (ebook)
Subjects: LCSH: Independence Hall (Philadelphia, Pa.)–Juvenile literature. | Philadelphia (Pa.)–Buildings, structures, etc.–Juvenile literature. | United States–Politics and government–1775-1783–Juvenile literature. | United States–Politics and government–1783-1789–Juvenile literature.
Classification: LCC F158.8.I3 L48 2025 (print) | LCC F158.8.I3 (ebook) | DDC 973.3–dc23/eng/20231205
LC record available at https://lccn.loc.gov/2023053528 LC ebook record available at https://lccn.loc.gov/2023053529

Published in 2025 by
Gareth Stevens Publishing
2544 Clinton Street
Buffalo, NY 14224

Designer: Tanya Dellaccio Keeney
Editor: Theresa Emminizer

Photo credits: Series background pixelparticle/Shutterstock.com; cover f11photo/Shutterstock.com; p. 5 dibrova/Shutterstock.com; p. 7 https://upload.wikimedia.org/wikipedia/commons/3/3b/The_Battle_of_Lexington.jpg; p. 9 (top) armoncheg/Shutterstock.com; p. 9 (bottom) Mark Krapels/Shutterstock.com; p. 11 (top) Courtesy of the National Park Service; p. 11 (bottom) https://upload.wikimedia.org/wikipedia/commons/d/d7/Portrait_of_George_III_by_Johann_Heinrich_von_Hurter.jpg; p. 13 (all) Everett Collection/Shutterstock.com; pp. 15, 17 (bottom), 19 (top) Courtesy of the National Archives; p. 17 (top) artnana/Shutterstock.com; p. 19 https://upload.wikimedia.org/wikipedia/commons/9/9d/Scene_at_the_Signing_of_the_Constitution_of_the_United_States.jpg.

Printed in the United States of America

CPSIA compliance information: Batch #CSGS25: For further information contact Gareth Stevens at 1-800-542-2595.

CONTENTS

Words in the glossary appear in **bold** type the first time they are used in the text.

WHAT IS INDEPENDENCE HALL?

Independence Hall is a famous building in Philadelphia, Pennsylvania. It's best known for events that happened during the American Revolution. You'll learn about that war in the next chapter.

Among the big events at Independence Hall were the signing of the **Declaration of Independence** and the **Constitution**. But those are just two of many important events that happened there. In this book, you'll discover the story of Independence Hall and its place in history.

INDEPENDENCE HALL HAS BEEN NAMED A WORLD **HERITAGE** SITE, OR LOCATION, IN HONOR OF ITS IMPORTANCE. IT'S ALSO KNOWN AS "THE BIRTHPLACE OF THE UNITED STATES."

KNOW THE FACTS!

NOT ALL EVENTS IN INDEPENDENCE HALL HELD GRAND IMPORTANCE. THE BASEMENT WAS ONCE USED AS PHILADELPHIA'S DOG POUND!

WHAT WAS THE AMERICAN REVOLUTION?

The American Revolution (1775–1783) was the war in which the British colonies won their freedom from England. But what caused it? England and its American colonies had existed together peacefully for almost 170 years before the war began.

The colonies had long been allowed to mostly rule themselves. But after the costly French and Indian War, the British government began to exercise more control over the colonies. England also ordered colonists pay costly new taxes. Colonists became angry and **rebelled**.

KNOW THE FACTS!

COLONISTS REALLY OBJECTED TO THE NEW TAXES PASSED BY THE BRITISH GOVERNMENT BECAUSE THEY HAD NO REPRESENTATIVES IN THAT GOVERNMENT. THEY CALLED THIS "TAXATION WITHOUT REPRESENTATION."

THE FIRST BATTLES OF THE AMERICAN REVOLUTION WERE FOUGHT AT LEXINGTON AND CONCORD IN MASSACHUSETTS ON APRIL 19, 1775.

THE BUILDING'S BEGINNING

Independence Hall didn't start out with that name or originally serve as a meeting place for representatives from the colonies. It started out as the Pennsylvania State House.

Philadelphia was the capital of the colony of Pennsylvania. Work began on the State House in 1732, and the government first met there in 1735. But the building wasn't completely finished until 1753. And it wasn't until 1824 that the building was called the Hall of Independence.

KNOW THE FACTS!

ALEXANDER HAMILTON, A PENNSYLVANIA GOVERNMENT LEADER AT THE TIME, CREATED THE FORM OF THE NEW STATE HOUSE. HE BECOME ONE OF THE **FOUNDING FATHERS** OF THE UNITED STATES.

THE FAMOUS LIBERTY BELL ORIGINALLY HUNG IN THE TOWER OF INDEPENDENCE HALL. IT WAS RUNG TO CALL GOVERNMENT LEADERS TO MEETINGS. IT WAS FIRST CALLED THE LIBERTY BELL IN 1835.

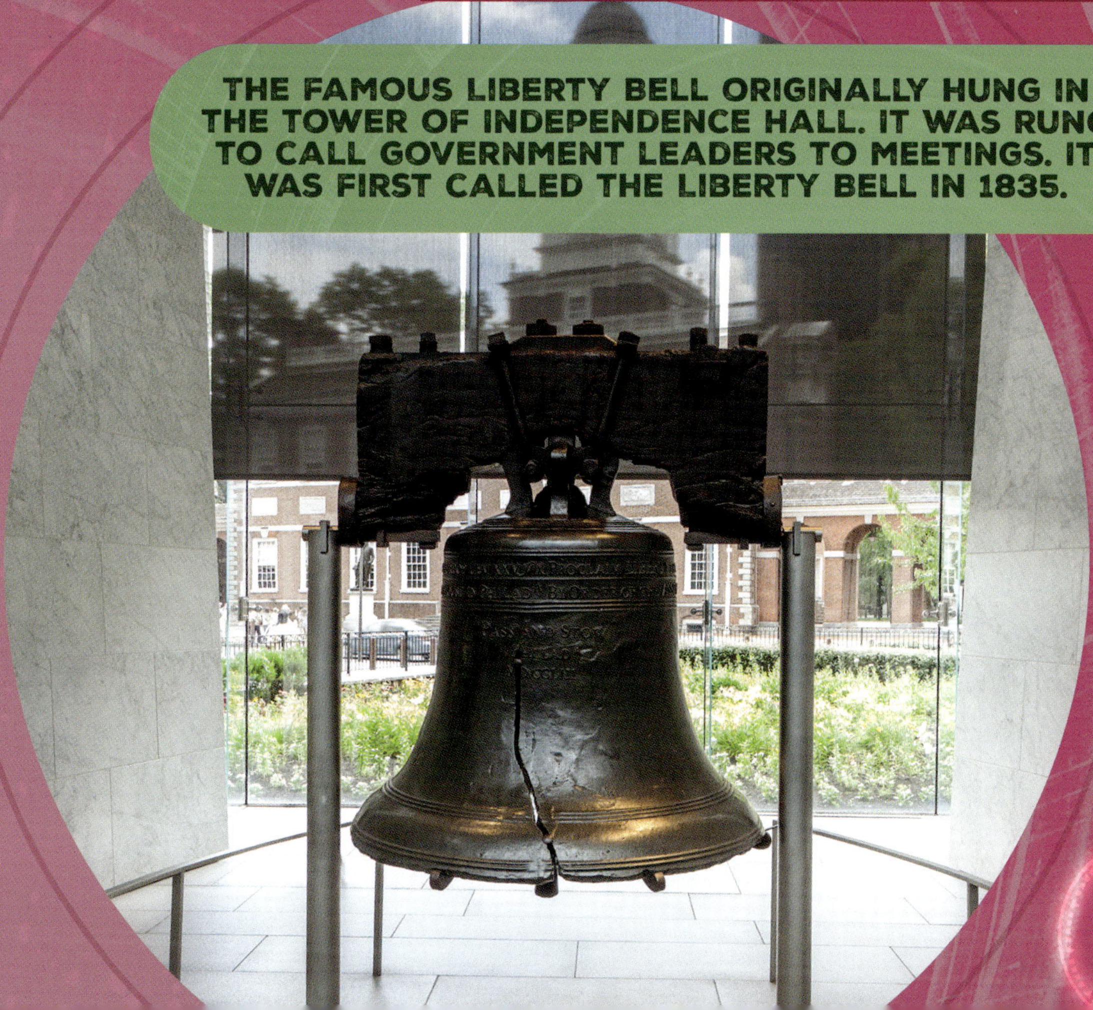

GETTING THE GANG TOGETHER

On May 10, 1775, representatives from the colonies gathered at Independence Hall in a meeting called the Second Continental Congress. The First Continental Congress had met in 1774 to try to peacefully address problems between the colonies and England. But by May 1775, the American Revolution had begun.

Members of the Congress decided to send a message to King George III in England trying to establish peace again. But they also knew they needed to get ready for war.

THIS IS THE ROOM IN INDEPENDENCE HALL WHERE THE SECOND CONTINENTAL CONGRESS MET AND MADE ITS IMPORTANT DECISIONS.

KNOW THE FACTS!

KING GEORGE III REFUSED TO ACCEPT THE PEACE MESSAGE FROM THE SECOND CONTINENTAL CONGRESS. HE WAS ANGRY AND SAID THE COLONIES WERE REBELLING AGAINST ENGLAND.

PREPARING TO FIGHT

The colonies weren't at all prepared to fight a mighty military force such as England. England had a powerful army and navy. The colonies had neither. Each colony had only a militia, made of ordinary citizens who fought when necessary.

So Congress formed a fighting force that would serve the united, or combined, colonies. It created the Continental Army on June 14, 1775, and appointed George Washington to lead it the next day. Congress created a navy on October 13, 1775.

John Adams

George Washington

THESE FOUNDING FATHERS WERE AMONG THE MEMBERS OF THE SECOND CONTINENTAL CONGRESS.

Thomas Jefferson

Patrick Henry

Samuel Adams

John Hancock

John Jay

Benjamin Franklin

KNOW THE FACTS!

ENGLAND HAD THE LARGEST NAVY IN THE WORLD WHEN THE AMERICAN REVOLUTION BEGAN. AT LEAST 50,000 BRITISH SOLDIERS FOUGHT IN THE WAR.

MAKING A STATEMENT

On June 7, 1776, Richard Henry Lee from Virginia presented a **resolution** to Congress. It said that "these United Colonies are, and of right ought to be, free and independent states." Congress agreed and appointed five men to write an official Declaration of Independence.

On July 2, 1776, Congress voted to declare, or announce, independence from England. On July 4, Congress adopted the Declaration of Independence. It had to be written on **parchment** before it could be signed. Signing began on August 2.

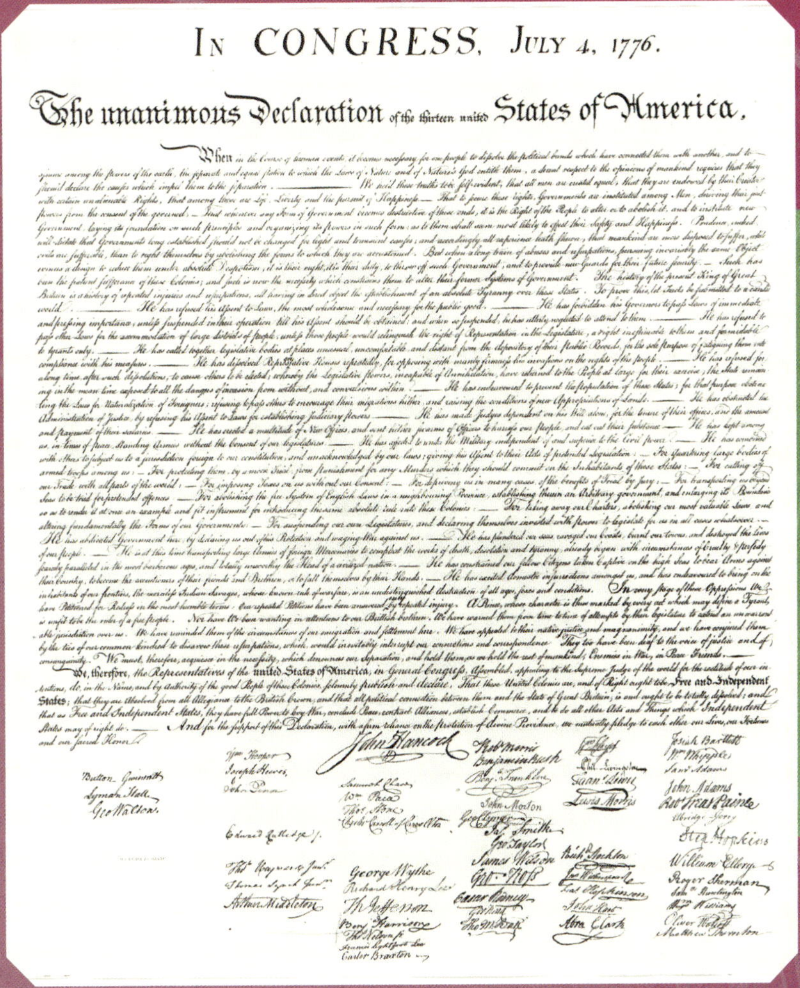

IN CONGRESS, JULY 4, 1776.

The unanimous Declaration of the thirteen united States of America.

SOME OF THE MOST FAMOUS WORDS FROM THE DECLARATION OF INDEPENDENCE ARE THESE: "WE HOLD THESE TRUTHS TO BE SELF-EVIDENT, THAT ALL MEN ARE CREATED EQUAL, THAT THEY ARE ENDOWED BY THEIR CREATOR WITH CERTAIN **UNALIENABLE** RIGHTS, THAT AMONG THESE ARE LIFE, LIBERTY AND THE PURSUIT OF HAPPINESS."

KNOW THE FACTS!

THE FIVE MEN APPOINTED TO WRITE THE DECLARATION WERE JOHN ADAMS, BENJAMIN FRANKLIN, ROGER SHERMAN, ROBERT R. LIVINGSTON, AND THOMAS JEFFERSON. JEFFERSON DID MOST OF THE WRITING.

SETTING UP A GOVERNMENT

If the colonies—which were now called states—were going to be independent from England, they needed to create a national government. At the same time Congress appointed men to write the Declaration of Independence, it appointed another group of men to figure out what this government would be like.

These men, led by John Dickinson of Delaware, wrote a constitution for the new, independent country. This constitution was called the Articles of Confederation. Congress adopted it on November 15, 1777.

THE ARTICLES OF CONFEDERATION ESTABLISHED A "LEAGUE OF FRIENDSHIP" AMONG THE 13 SOVEREIGN AND INDEPENDENT STATES. THIS MEANT THE STATES HELD MOST OF THE POWER AND THE NATIONAL GOVERNMENT HELD VERY LITTLE POWER.

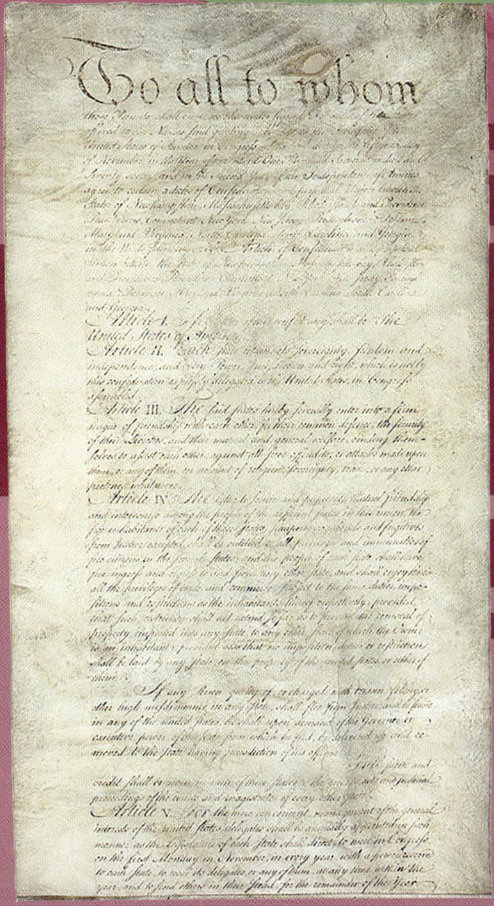

To all to whom

KNOW THE FACTS!

EACH STATE HAD TO RATIFY, OR AGREE TO, THE ARTICLES OF CONFEDERATION BEFORE THE NEW CONSTITUTION WENT INTO EFFECT. THIS DIDN'T HAPPEN UNTIL MARCH 1, 1781.

FIXING THE GOVERNMENT

It soon became clear the Articles' government plan wasn't working. The young nation was in danger of falling apart. So Congress called a meeting to address the problems.

Led by George Washington, representatives gathered in Independence Hall from May 25 to September 17, 1787. They tried to make changes to the Articles of Confederation, but soon realized the Articles couldn't be fixed. They drew up a whole new government plan. It became the Constitution, and the meeting came to be called the Constitutional Convention.

KNOW THE FACTS!

CONGRESS APPROVED THE CONSTITUTION ON SEPTEMBER 17, 1787. BUT AT LEAST NINE STATES HAD TO RATIFY IT FOR IT TO BECOME LAW. NEW HAMPSHIRE BECAME THE NINTH STATE ON JUNE 21, 1788.

We the People

Article. 1

THE CONSTITUTION BEGINS WITH THESE IMPORTANT WORDS: "WE THE PEOPLE OF THE UNITED STATES, IN ORDER TO FORM A MORE PERFECT UNION, ESTABLISH JUSTICE, INSURE DOMESTIC **TRANQUILITY**, PROVIDE FOR THE COMMON DEFENCE, PROMOTE THE GENERAL WELFARE, AND SECURE THE BLESSINGS OF LIBERTY TO OURSELVES AND OUR **POSTERITY**, DO ORDAIN AND ESTABLISH THIS CONSTITUTION FOR THE UNITED STATES OF AMERICA."

INDEPENDENCE HALL TODAY

Today, Independence Hall is part of Independence National Historical Park. Although the building has been changed several times over the years, today it looks much as it did during the American Revolution and the early years of the new nation.

Visitors to Independence Hall can see the room where the Second Continental Congress and Constitutional Convention met. They can see the chair George Washington sat in during the Convention. Over 2 1/2 million people visit Independence Hall each year—and you can too!

THIS TIMELINE LISTS SOME OF THE MOST IMPORTANT EVENTS THAT TOOK PLACE AT INDEPENDENCE HALL.

May 10, 1775	The Second Continental Congress begins meeting there.
June 14, 1775	Congress forms the Continental Army.
June 15, 1775	George Washington is named leader of the army.
October 13, 1775	Congress forms the navy.
June 7, 1776	Richard Henry Lee presents his resolution to Congress.
July 2, 1776	Congress votes to declare independence from England.
July 4, 1776	Congress adopts the Declaration of Independence.
November 15, 1777	Congress adopts the Articles of Confederation.
May 25, 1787	The Constitutional Convention begins.
September 17, 1787	Congress approves the Constitution.

KNOW THE FACTS!

THE LIBERTY BELL IS NO LONGER IN INDEPENDENCE HALL'S TOWER. IT'S BEEN MOVED TO A PLACE IN THE PARK CALLED LIBERTY BELL CENTER, WHERE IT'S EASY TO VISIT.

GLOSSARY

constitution: The basic laws by which a country or state is governed.

Declaration of Independence: The piece of writing in which the colonies said they were free from British rule.

Founding Father: One of the men who played an important part in creating the U.S. government.

heritage: Something that comes from past members of a family or group.

parchment: An old kind of paper made from the skins of sheep or goats.

posterity: People who will live after someone.

rebel: To fight to overthrow a government.

representative: One who stands for a group of people. Also, a member of a lawmaking body who acts for voters.

resolution: An official statement of purpose voted on by a group.

sovereign: Having independent authority and the right to govern itself.

tranquility: The quality of being peaceful.

unalienable: Not capable of being taken away.

FOR MORE INFORMATION

Books

Carr, Aaron. *Independence Hall*. New York, NY: AV2, 2022.

Gunderson, Jessica. *Independence Hall: All About the American Symbol*. North Mankato, MN: Pebble, 2021.

Websites

Independence Hall: 1756
https://bensguide.gpo.gov/j-independence-hall
Read more about Independence Hall on this website.

Independence Hall in American Memory
www.independencehall-americanmemory.com/timeline/
Here you can find a timeline of all the important events that have happened at Independence Hall.

INDEX